THE ANTIQUES JOKESHOW

JOKES FROM THE ATTIC

ROY CHUBBY BROWN

WITH
GEORGE PROUDMAN

ILLUSTRATIONS BY ROY CHUBBY BROWN

Published in paperback in 2017 by Sixth Element Publishing
on behalf of Roy Chubby Brown and George Proudman

© Roy Chubby Brown and George Proudman 2017

ISBN 978-1-912218-12-7

British Library Cataloguing in Publication Data. A catalogue record for this book is available from the British Library.

All rights reserved. No part of this publication may be reproduced, stored in a retrieval system or transmitted, in any form or by any means, electronic, mechanical, photocopying, recording and/or otherwise without the prior written permission of the publishers. This book may not be lent, resold, hired out or disposed of by way of trade in any form, binding or cover other than that in which it is published without the prior written consent of the publishers.

Roy Chubby Brown and George Proudman assert the moral right to be identified as the authors of this work.

Printed in Great Britain.

CONTENTS

Foreword by Bobby Ball 1

Introduction 3

Chubby's Comedy Crèche 5

Knock, Knock, Who's There? 9

Back At School 17

Home Sweet Home 21

Little Old Me 24

Doctor I'm In Trouble 26

Fat Not Fit 28

Our Lass 31

Police Farce 37

At The Shops 39

Men At Work 42

Things I Can't Stand 44

Box Of Tricks 45

Heard It Down The Pub 48

My Old Flames 50

Summertime Blues 53

Our Lass 55

Mr. Allcock & Mr. Brown 61

My Old Mate 62

Football Crazy	65
Home Sweet Home	69
Greasy Spoon	71
Sex Cymbal	73
It's A Dog's Life	76
Grub Up	78
The Fairer Sex	80
Technophobia	82
Our Lass	84
Police Farce	88
Random	91
Mr. Allcock & Mr. Brown	94
Things I Can't Stand	95
My Old Flames	96
Heard It Down The Pub	101
Doctor I'm In Trouble	104
Attila The Mother-in-Law	106
Little Old Me	110
Brass Monkeys	113
Mam & Dad	115
Police Farce	119
Our Lass	122
Sex Cymbal	127

Mr. Allcock & Mr. Brown	131
There's A Bloke In Our Pub	133
Home Sweet Home	136
Heard It Down The Pub	138
Doctor I'm In Trouble	140
Jack The Lad	142
My Old Flames	145
The Most Wonderful Time Of The Year	148
Our Lass	149
Sex Cymbal	153
Mr. Allcock & Mr. Brown	156
Not So Little Drummer Boy	158
There's No Business Like Show Business	165
Things I Can't Stand	168
Doctor I'm In Trouble	169
Home Sweet Home	171
Things I Can't Stand	174
Little Old Me	175

FOREWORD

I have known Roy Chubby Brown at least thirty years and have heard about him for even longer.

There's a fact, that not a lot of people are aware of, there's a difference between a comic and a comedian. A comedian tells funny stories, whereas a comic is a funny man. Yes, a comic makes you smile inside, as soon as he steps on stage, without even opening his mouth.

Roy Chubby Brown is a comic, and it is my honour to know him and count him as a friend. There are many comics and comedians, but there is only one Roy Chubby Brown.

Bobby Ball x

INTRODUCTION

How many times do you hear someone say, "aye, the old jokes are the best," or "there's nothing like an old joke." Well, here's a fucking book load of them, together with a handful of tall stories. Now, don't you be complaining 'cos I'm sure you've said it yourself. Anyway look on the bright side, if you found it funny the first time then you should laugh at it again. On the other hand, you might not have got it when you heard it the first time, so, on the other hand... oh fuck, that's three hands isn't it? Well, on the other bollock, you might just think the joke's a load of shit and not funny at all. You see, you can't please all of the people all of the time... by, there aren't half some miserable bastards out there.

As I'm sure you all know, I work like fuck every day to dream up new material for my shows and DVDs. So over the years I've accumulated a lot of old jokes, some of which haven't seen the light of day since Adam was a lad... '♫ Who the fuck's Adam? ♫' (to the tune of Alice). Ha ha!

I expect some of you will be thinking I've written this book especially for that thick bloke who came up to me in a club shit-house and said, "Why, you've a canny act young 'un (it was a long time ago), but can't yer tell us a joke we know?" But no, I haven't, it's especially for you, my loyal fan. The one who has supported me all these years through the good jokes and the bad, the one who lives in a phone box in Redcar. Yes, I'm talking about you, the one who'd laugh if his, or her, fucking arse was on fire and then come back year after year for more.

So to show my appreciation, I've collected together a selection of the jokes you've been laughing at over the years. Some you'll remember, some you won't. Some you'll laugh like fuck at, and some you won't. Some you might even have missed. There'll be some you'll think, 'What the fuck is he on about?' and then get it later.

Because of the adult content of most of my jokes, we thought we had better leave some of the underage stuff in what we've called our 'Comedy Crèche'. It's at the beginning of the book and there are a few cracks in there that you can tell to the next generation of Chubby fans.

So sit back and relax, brace yourself and please enjoy a nostalgic trip back in time to when your mate Chubby used to get paid off and barred out of some of the country's biggest workingmen's clubs just for telling some of the jokes you are about to read.

One last request though, loyal fan… when you turn each page over, please remember to blow all of the fucking cobwebs off as you go.

Yours forever,
Chubbs x

CHUBBY'S COMEDY CRÈCHE

How come a birthday cake is the only thing you can blow and spit on yet everyone still wants a fucking slice?

What's tall, pointy and made from custard, cake and jelly?

The fucking Trifle Tower, of course.

What's the brainiest fish in the sea?

Halibut Einstein, clever twat.

Two flies playing football on a saucer when one of them said, "We'll have to play better than this next week, we're playing in the fucking cup."

My pet piglet's just like his dad… he's a chop off the old block.

Two eggs boiling in a pan… one egg says,
"Fuck me it's hot in here, isn't it?"

The other egg says, "You're dead right, mate, but wait till you get out, they bash your bastard brains in."

What do you call a bear with no mam or dad?

Rupert the bastard.

What do you call a gorilla with a machine gun?

Fuck all if you know what's good for you.

Why did the dinosaur cross the road?

Because there were no fucking chickens in those days.

If the milkman brings the milk, the coalman brings the coal, and the postman brings the post… what does the bogeyman bring?

KNOCK, KNOCK, WHO'S THERE?

"Push, Mrs. Vasey, push. We're nearly there."

It's Saturday 3rd February 1945.

"I am fucking pushing," came the reply. "What do you think I'm doing, you fat old twat?" (Now you know where I get it from) was the answer to the midwife's obvious instructions. "Where's my miserable sod of a husband?"

Midwife replies, "He rang the hospital to say he's been asked to do a double at work, he'll see you tomorrow. Anyway keep pushing, Mrs. Vasey," she added, quite nervously.

"Ayeeeeeee!" Another scream from me mam, followed by, "Double? I'll give him fucking double when I see him, he'll be in that fucking Unity Club with his mates, ayeeeeeeeee!"

Dad thought it was most inconvenient of me mam to go into labour on a Saturday, the same night of the week when he had his usual piss up with his mates in the club. Aye, dad couldn't let his mates' weekly dominoes school down, whatever the reason.

For the younger reader, dominos school doesn't mean they were learning how to make fucking pizzas, just so you know. No, dominoes – doms as they were affectionately known – was a type of religion among the working men in North East clubs and it was taken very seriously, but they had to be careful in the Unity Club, because, as I'm sure you all know, if you can't 'go' in the game of doms, you knock quite loudly on the table. Now, whenever this happened, the rest of the lads in the bar would dive for cover under the nearest table. You see, in Grangetown, the only time you heard knocking was if the police were at your front door, or, worse still, the rent man. So the only double me dad had in mind when he rang the hospital was probably a double six.

"Keep pushing, Mrs. Vasey, we can see his cap."

Everyone's a comic. In those days, you didn't know if you were having a boy or a girl till they popped out.

"Ayeeeee, I'll never let that baldy bastard of a husband near me again," screamed me mam.

"One more push, one more push, the head's out."

"Ayeeeee, yah fucker!"

"Here we go, Mrs. Vasey, you've got a bouncing baby boy."

I remember putting that on my CV when I applied to be a ball-boy for my local football team.

"Well stop fucking bouncing him then," me mam blasted.

"Yes, he's a big lad," said the midwife as everyone in the delivery room started chanting, "You fat bastard! You fat bastard!"

How did they know it was me?

Back at the Unity Club, dad's still unaware that he's

become a father for the first time, not that fathers had too much to do with bringing their kids up in those days. Their main role in life being to administer corporal punishment by means of a smack round the head when you least expected it, whether you deserved one or not.

"Wonder if anything's happened yet, Colin," one of the lads remarked to me dad.

"Where have they taken her?" asked another.

"Parkhurst,' replied dad.

"Parkhurst's a prison, yer daft sod, you must mean Parkside, the Maternity Hospital beside the park."

'Well, I'm not sure," said dad. "She wants fucking locking up."

Mam and dad used to fight like fuck. I don't know how they managed to have me and my sister, Barbara. I really don't.

"Haven't a clue," continued dad. "I'll find out in the morning. Now who's fucking round is it?"

By this time mam has been handed her bouncing baby boy so that she can get to know me.

"Have you thought of a name yet, Mrs. Vasey?"

"Yes," she said, "he's going to be called Royston, so that we can shorten it to Roy, after Roy Rogers, my favourite actor."

"Very nice," said the attending nurse and promptly put a sign on my cradle saying 'Roy the Boy'. I suppose if I'd been a girl, I'd have been called Pearl. My mother didn't have much of an imagination.

So that's how I think I must have entered the world, with me mam screaming like fuck in Parkhurst, I mean, Parkside, and me dad at the club playing doms and getting pissed off his face with his mates. Start as you mean to go on, me dad always said, so while I was still in the hospital, I nicked another baby's bottle of milk (only joking, I didn't master the art of thieving till much later in life).

We lived in a two up, two down terraced house in Grangetown. Life hadn't been easy for the local people. The war hadn't yet finished and we were sandwiched between Dorman Long Steel Works, where me dad worked, and ICI, where you worked if you'd passed the 11 plus. Yes, anyone who worked at ICI came home from work looking like they'd just got out of the bath, where as steel workers, even on their way to work, looked like they hadn't seen a bar of fucking soap for six months, the muck was so ingrained. You could always tell the steel workers from the ICI workers at the grand social night out of the week – a Saturday night at the local workies – their caps were a different shade of filth.

The heavy industry in the area, together with the docks, meant it was a prime target for Hitler's bombs. Our family had been one of the lucky ones with an Anderson shelter at the bottom of the yard. An Anderson shelter was built of corrugated iron, shaped to deflect any shrapnel flying from bombs that might have landed nearby. Mind you, a direct hit and you were fucked anyway. Family folklore has it that me dad would never go to the shelter when the sirens sounded. He would just sit on the settee in the living room and not budge an inch. His voice would always boom out, "If that bomb's got your name on it, there's no hiding place. It'll get you wherever you are." That was okay for our family to hear, but not much comfort for our neighbours, Mr. & Mrs. Doodlebug.

Accompanying the Anderson shelter, which stayed up for many years after it was needed, at the bottom of the yard was the outside toilet. It had a wooden seat and I remember every time me dad went to the toilet, he would say, "Just going down to the bog for a spell," with his copy of the Daily Mirror tucked under his arm, even in the fucking dark. Never really understood that one until one day I realised the paper had a few pages less when he came back. There were always sheets from yesterday's paper cut into squares and hung up on a nail in the outside bog anyway. I often went to school on a Monday with the weekend's football results imprinted on the cheeks of my arse. Some of the lads in my class would bring their dad's pools coupons to school and check them off at playtime while I stood in a corner of the playground with my kecks round my ankles.

Because the toilet was outside, we always had to have other receptacles in the house in case anyone wanted to go during the night. When I was a little bit older, I'd started getting interested in girls and I fancied this girl something rotten. It took me ages to build up the courage to ask her out. Surprisingly she said yes, so I took her to the pictures to see 'Moby Dick', I think.

Afterwards, knowing that mam and dad would be in bed, I took her back to our house, hoping it would lead to something I hadn't yet done. We crept quietly into the house which had a long passage with a door leading into the living room. Just before the stairs at the far end, I said, "Don't switch the light on." She obviously thought it was so we wouldn't attract attention, but it was really so she wouldn't see that there was no light bulb in, and hadn't been for some years.

As we tiptoed along the passage, which these days even I would be calling 'a hall', how times have changed, I caught my shin on the pedal of my dad's rusty old bike and tried to stifle a cry but couldn't stop a pathetic whimper from escaping. Hey, a bike covered in rust, oil and probably dog-shit leaning against the wallpaper of the passage/hall, a tradition that's disappeared from the modern household, I'm sure. Oh, not all households, I hear you say.

"Is that you, our Roy?" me mam shouted from upstairs.

My whimper must have been louder than I thought. Rather reluctantly I answered her back, "Yes, mam, it's me."

"Oh good, you're just in time," she replied, 'fetch the bucket up, son, your dad wants a shite."

My shoulders dropped and I turned to see the dark shadow of my beautiful date speeding towards the front door, catching her brand new 21 denier stockings on a stray spoke sticking out from the front wheel of me dad's bike in her rush to get out.

"Fuck me," she cried, "first time on too."

Then the front door opened with the street lighting bouncing off the fabulous shape of her navy blue gabardine Mac, the door slammed shut and she disappeared into the night never to be seen again.

I was still there in the dark, at the bottom of our stairs with my mouth wide open wondering what the fuck had just happened, a voice in my head reminding me, 'Still a virgin, then?' when I was brought out of my trance by a thunderous voice from upstairs, "Roy, get a fucking move on, your dad's got a tortoise's head," mam again ever so eloquently, "and don't forget the Daily Mirror!"

BACK AT SCHOOL

We had some characters at our school. I remember one who'd come to school with the arse hanging out of his pants, nose always running, shirt hanging out, and his breakfast down the front of his jumper. Yes, a funny fucking headmaster he was.

I was recently talking to an old school friend. He said, "Remember that girl behind the bike sheds, she was good wasn't she? But not as good as our lass."

I said, "Yeah, you're dead right, mate, she wasn't as good as your lass."

He said, "I've got ten kids now."

I said, "Oh I've only got the one, I used me head."

He said, "Fucking hell, Chubby, that must have hurt your ears."

The lad next to me at school was always smoking.
I used to set him on fire.

When I bumped into another old pal, I said, "Haven't seen you since we were at school, how's life been treating you?"

"Oh," he said, "I got into music when I left school, played the drums in a local band, met a girl who plays the piano and got married. We had two kids, one plays the violin and the other plays the saxophone. Pop round one night and we'll have a musical evening. What have you been doing, Chubby?"

I said, "I got into trouble, got sent to borstal for GBH, when I came out I went to kick-boxing lessons, met a girl there and we got married. Funnily enough, I've got two kids as well, one does karate and the other one's a boxer. Pop round one night and we'll give you a fucking good hiding."

A girl pissed herself in our class. The teacher said, "Why didn't you put your hand up?"

The girl said, "I did, miss, but it ran through me fingers."

The teacher said to me one day, "Chubby, I think it's time that me and you had a talk about girls."

I said, "Okay, sir, what do you want to know?"

I was standing outside the school when a policeman came up to me and said, "You're loitering, son, you must be up to no good."

I said, "I am not. A fella told me to mind that dog shit and he hasn't come back yet."

I was so unpopular at school that my best friend was the nit-nurse.

I'm like you, I got my sex education at school where they'd treat us like fucking idiots. It wasn't like it is today. One teacher brought in a bag of jelly babies and said, "You can tell the boy ones from the girl ones, because the boy ones have a little bit more jelly on them." After that, the first time I went out with a girl I tried to bite her fucking head off.

Teacher said, "Have you fallen out with me, son. You've been bringing me a big bag of raisins in every day for the last year and now you've suddenly stopped?"

I said, "Me rabbit's dead, miss."

I came home from school once looking a bit down in the dumps. My dad said, "What's up, son?"

I said, "Kids at school keep calling me big head."

Dad said, "You take no notice of the kids in your school, son, they're just being spiteful. Now do me a big favour and go and get your mam two stone of potatoes from the shop."

I said, "Okay, dad, but what shall I carry them in?"

He said, "Just use your fucking cap."

We were doing geography at school and the teacher said to little Tommy, "Where's the Nigerian border, Tommy?"

Tommy said, "He's at home in bed with me mam, Miss."

HOME SWEET HOME

Our greedy bastard dad got double-glazing
so we couldn't hear the ice-cream van.

We had to drink our own urine in a glass so the
neighbours thought we could afford orange juice.

When we were kids, we were so poor we had to use
stick-on soles. No shoes, just stick-on soles.

My mother wasn't a brilliant cook, and money was
tight too. So at dinnertime there was always trouble if
any of us kids dared to ask for an extra slice of gravy.

The landlord called at our house one day and
said to me dad, "I heard you were looking for me.
What do you want me for?"

Me dad said, "It's about the roof."

The landlord said, "What about the roof?"

Me dad said, "We'd just like one."

I'm so lazy. I won't get out of the bath for a piss.

Then our neighbours are so posh that they don't piss in the bath, they do it into a sponge and squeeze it down the sink.

I used to love it when grandma took me for a piss 'cos her hand used to shake.

There is such a bad breath problem where I live that everyone mouthwashes with raw sewage.

My dad was hard. I tell you, he was so hard he survived an abortion.

It's so promiscuous in our town that most of the kids lose their virginity before their mothers do.

It is such a rough area the ice cream van has a bouncer, the Jehovah's witness fuck all, bought an advent calendar and all the windows were broken, the postman delivers letters soaked in blood, the vicar at the church said some cunt's pinched the swear box. Policewomen slash car tyres.

Our friends are so rough that when they come to dinner we have to count the knives and forks.

The air conditioning's knackered... the bat's died.

Me dad always used to say, "Fight fire with fire." He got kicked out of the Fire Brigade.

LITTLE OLD ME

Wearing a cap makes me tired. It's a fucking night-cap.

I call my wife's fanny a stamp because I like to lick it.

I got fourteen presents for my birthday…
seven pairs of fucking socks.

I've had my suit since it was a pair of bastard gloves.

The wife said, "You've got a big drip
on the end of your nose.'

I put the back of my hand up to the
end of my nose and said, "I have not."

She said, "No, the other end."… cheeky bastard.

The swimming baths were so crowded that I had to dive in three times before I hit any water.

Last night I worked with a Chinese comedian called On Too Long, and fucking hell, was he.

I'm as sick as a giraffe with fucking vertigo.

I've decided to give up pork pies. If my wife can give up smoking, then I should be able to give up pork pies. So I'm going to do what she did when she first gave up smoking, I'm just going to have one after each meal… and two after sex.

My previous marriage was like a fucking prison sentence. No, I tell a lie, I got more sex when I was in jail.

DOCTOR I'M IN TROUBLE

I went to the doctors. He said, "Come in and take all of your clothes off."

I said, "Oh, where shall I put them?"

He said, "Next to mine."

Then he said, "I want you to wee in that glass.'

I said, "What, from here?"

Sticky Vicky went to her Gynaecologist complaining of a pain in her fanny. He said, "I think you might have picked something up."

I had to have an operation last week. That keyhole surgery's fantastic, the surgeon came to my house and didn't even have to open the front door.

I came around in hospital and the doctor said, "What's the nurse given you?"

"Oh," I said, "the nurse hasn't given me anything, doctor, I think I must have caught it off that mucky tart I slept with last weekend."

The doctor said, "I'll examine you for two quid."

I said, "That's good of you, doctor. If you find two quid, I'll split it with you… we'll have a quid each."

Went to the doctor's yesterday and told him, "Every time I sneeze I get a hard on."

He said, "Are you taking anything for it?"

I said, "Yes, pepper."

"Excuse me, doctor, I think I'm invisible."

"Who the fuck said that?"

FAT NOT FIT

I was out jogging when a man on a fucking
lawn mower overtook me.

I love the second week of dieting
'cos by then I've packed the twat in.

Dieting makes you moody, irritable and nasty,
but that also happens if you tell a fat person
he can't have any chips.

Not only can I not fit into my trousers, these days
I can't even fit into the fucking changing rooms.

He thinks a balanced diet is a hamburger in each hand.

I'm overdrawn at the foodbank.

You are what you eat. I must be a cunt.

She said, "I'm into a twelve now."

I said, "What in? A fucking shoe?"

I've realised that getting fat makes
your dick look smaller.

I'm on a diet at the moment. When I weigh myself on a morning, I make sure I don't have a hard on, 'cos I think you weigh more with a hard on.

Just finished my first marathon,
got a Mars Bar for later on. *(Jog on!)*

Every morning it's 'up one two, down one two'…
then the other sock.

OUR LASS

Didn't have a dog…
for years the wife bit the postman.

Our lass can't change her knickers
'cos she left the fucking tyre lever in the garage.

If she had a facelift, they'd have to hire
a forklift truck from the docks.

Wife said, "£50.00 for a sexy bra?
I'll let them swing first."

The wife just bought a Xmas cake and it wasn't
until she got it home that she noticed it said,
'Use by 24th December 2017'.

I married her 'cos I'd never heard anybody
who could fart as loud as me before.

She sleeps with her hand on her fanny
so I can't help myself during the night.

If I'd fucked as many women as my wife thinks I have,
I'd be first in the queue at the AIDS clinic.

She says I'm lazy and don't buy her anything just
because she tore her wedding dress hod-carrying.

It was an offensive t-shirt.
Well, it was when she wore it.

Our lass said she's thinking of having a fanny tuck.
I said, "Don't bother, you have a fanny tuck every
night… you tuck it away so I can't fucking get at it."

NOW YOUR IN A (COO) MOO!)
CAN I HAVE A RISE IN MY HOUSE KEEPING!

Doctor's told me I've only fourteen fucks left in my penis. Told the wife but she said unfortunately my name's not on her bucket list. Then I thought, 'Yeah, that's about the fucking size of it.'

😃

Got my own back last night,
I dipped her vibrator in Tabasco sauce.

😆

Kids accidentally dropped the wife's tampons in the bog, now there's no water left in the bowl.

😜

I said, "Fancy a bit, dear?"

"No, I've got a headache."

"That wasn't the end I was thinking about."

😂

We had a sunken bath but only when she got in it.

😆

Our lass is so hard-faced that she laughs like fuck
when she's chopping raw onions.

😂

Wife said, "I've bought another mouse trap,
the one I bought yesterday is full."

😜

Our son was born at an awkward time...
ruined the fucking honeymoon

😂

I brought some flowers in for the wife.
She said, "I suppose I'll have to
open my legs for them, won't I?"

I said, "Haven't you bought a fucking vase yet?"

😆

Didn't get any tea yesterday...
the wife burnt the salad.

😜

The wife went out dressed to kill this morning.
Mind you, she does work at the abattoir.

😃

The wife and I were cuddling in bed when I said,
"Kiss me on the fore…" and she gave me a smacker
right in the middle of my head just above my eyes,
before I could say, "skin."

😆

Strange if you see another woman's fanny you'd get
excited. If you see the wife's, you don't even look up.

😜

The wife got dressed this morning, I said,
"Are you going trick or treating?"

😂

Then she was a bed tester and got sacked
for lying down on the job.

😃

POLICE FARCE

I should have been a policeman.
I'm always helping them with their fucking enquiries.

I went to prison for something I didn't do.
I didn't get to the fucking car fast enough.

I stopped one from drowning too.
I took my foot off his fucking head.

I should have only got six months but I was up
at court on a Sunday and it was double time.

The prisoner shouted, "Warden,
it's fucking freezing in this cell."

The warden replied,
"Okay, I'll put you another bar on."

All I'd done was borrow some money off a mate of mine. Mind you, he was asleep at the time.

I was in jail for two years and the wife never looked at another man for fucking days.

I'd been reported for a hit-and-run accident. I said, "Fuck off, the chap never looked both ways."

The copper said, "Why should he? He was stood in his own front room."

I got caught stealing from the library. My solicitor's told me they'll probably throw the book at me.

Police were called to a woman who claimed she had been attacked by a man with an e-cigarette… they said it's the first case they've had of anyone being vaped.

AT THE SHOPS

I went into the chemist and said to the assistant, "A box of condoms please, miss."

She said quite abruptly, "Don't you 'miss' me."

So I said, "Better make that two boxes then."

Knocked a display counter down in Poundland and caused four pounds worth of fucking damage.

No such thing as free-range eggs.
Chickens aren't free, you never see them queuing up for a ride at Alton Towers.

The attendant at the fitting rooms in Matalan told her boss, "There's a man in here keeps coming back to the fitting room with the same jacket every ten minutes."

Her boss said, "Watch him very carefully, he's been in here before, I'm sure he's trying it on."

I got a phone call from the toy shop saying the cheque
I gave them for the trampoline had fucking bounced.

😆

Granddaughter's just had twins. She wanted to name
them after the place where they were conceived.
So she called one Mat and the other one Alan,
'cos they were conceived in a Matalan fitting room.

🤪

"Excuse me, can I try those trousers
on in the window?"

Assistant replies, "Only if you want everyone
in the street to stop and watch you."

😂

Written on the side of a tampon box:
in case of damp, pull string.

😃

I've just doubled the value of my car,
I've left the shopping in the boot.

🤪

Been shopping looking for a new arse,
but they've all got cracks in them.

We've a new supermarket opened near us
especially for senior citizens. It's called Oldi.

I went into the chemist shop this morning and
bought the biggest box of Durex Extra-Sensitive
condoms I could find. I didn't need any, I just wanted
to see the look on the pretty girl assistant's face
when I put them on the counter.

Sign in a shop window…
'Ears pierced while you wait.'

When you're on the motorway there are always
signs when you're coming up to the services like
'Tiredness Can Kill' or 'Take A Break.'

Well, on the A1 there's an Adults Only Superstore,
and there should be a sign about a mile
before it saying, 'Need a Wank?'

MEN AT WORK

He's never had a day's illness in his life…
always makes it last a whole fucking week.

But he did have two weeks off work once
with a broken flask.

We call him jigsaw 'cos if you
mention work he goes to pieces.

It appears that there are illegal immigrants
in our area that have been employed by local
farmers to look after sheep. My brother has been
asked to work undercover to try and find them.
He's been employed as a Shepherd's spy.

At one job that I had there were both lads and lasses
working there. Our boss was a lesbian and the girls
were always her favourites, us lads used to have bets
on which one of the girls was going to be the next
one fingered for promotion.

I was the son of a bricklayer. Mother had to take any work she could get after the war.

A mate of mine works in a public toilet, he told me that he's sick of perverts and druggies using the place all of the time. He said a bloke came in the other day for a shit and it was like a breath of fresh air.

You know my brother's always looking down on me. I blame his new job… he's a steeplejack.

When I was a painter and decorator, I was asked to go and redecorate a local brothel. When I got there it was so busy that the girls had fuck all on and wouldn't move out of the way for me, so I ended up just papering over the cracks.

A bunch of male prostitutes have opened up a website to advertise themselves… they've called it Bumtree.

THINGS I CAN'T STAND

People who call their kids Cruise or Apple.

😀

Women who only let you put the head in.

😜

Siamese twins with only one fanny.

😆

Sex change men who go from
daddy to mummy in 24 hours.

🤣

When you're told that your face
would cure sex offenders.

😀

Fanny farts.

😜

BOX OF TRICKS

I used to be a boxer. I had twenty eight professional fights. Lost one, drew two and chickened out of twenty fucking five.

😂

When I climbed into the ring for my first fight, all the women in the crowd screamed. I was that nervous I'd forgotten to put my shorts on.

😆

I used to box under the name of Rembrandt, because I was always on the canvas.

😜

When I fought one bloke, I'd have had to knock him out just to get a draw. But let me tell you, he was covered in blood alright… mine.

😃

I was on my back so many times during a fight that firms used to battle with each other to see who could get the advertising space on the soles of my boots.

😃

I boxed one fellow and it started out really well. I cut him above the eye, I cut him above the ear, cut him above the nose. Then the ref stopped the fight and took the razor blade off me.

😂

Another bastard hit me so hard
I had to pay to get back in.

😆

My corner said to me, "Listen, you've got him here, he hasn't laid a glove on you."

I said, "Well keep an eye on the ref 'cos someone's knocking ten colours of shite out of me in there."

🤪

My problem was I was all heart. If I ever knocked someone over, I'd forgive them for falling down.

I was a boxer when I left school…
I used to box oranges.

I went to kick-boxing lessons and learnt how to knock a bloke out with my bare feet. I remember coming home from the pub one night when two lads set on me and knocked shit out of me while I was getting my fucking shoes and socks off.

Trainer to a boxer, "When I said 'hit him with all you've got', I didn't mean the fucking stool as well."

Wife's been buying me boxer shorts instead of budgie smugglers. I've asked her to stop buying me boxers because my willy slips down the right side and catches on my accelerator pedal when I'm driving.

HEARD IT DOWN THE PUB

They are selling drugs on our estate… thank fuck.

Wonder what Sylvester Stallone's mother will do when her looks go.

Never say to an Irishman, "Top of the morning," unless you want a knuckle sandwich.

Dylan got the Nobel Prize In Literature… come a long way since The Magic Roundabout.

What's the most common sign you'll see on the motorway?

'Pick Your Own Strawberries'

They've found bones on the moon...
the cow can't have jumped high enough.

Blind man picked up the cheese grater and said,
"That's the best book I've ever read."

This fellow pulled a razor on me...
good job it wasn't plugged in.

I must have been drunk 'cos on the way home
people kept standing on my fingers.

An Argos delivery van pulled up alongside me in the street and the driver wound the window down and said, "Do you know what time it is, mate?"

I said, "Not sure, pal, somewhere between eight in the morning and four in the afternoon."

See how he fucking likes it.

MY OLD FLAMES (DIRTY BITCHES)

Met a girl last night, I said, "What's your name?"

She said, "Jenny."

I said, "That's a nice name."

She said, "Yes it's short for Genitalia, some of my friends call me Fanny."

It's only puppy love 'cos she keeps licking me behind the ears and sniffing my arse.

Bumped into an old girl friend, I said, "What have you been doing?"

She said, "Having your baby."

She might be a blind prostitute but you've got to hand it to her.

She said, "I'm only thirteen."

I said, "I'm not superstitious."

😆

She said, "Do you think I'm pretty?"

I said, "How many guesses have I got?"

😜

She gets drunk on water, she gets drunk on land.

😂

She was covered in bruises where the lads
had touched her with a twelve-foot barge pole.

I was a bit peeved when I saw she had
three bikers' names tattooed on her arse.

😃

I knew she wouldn't like my act when
she told me the dog had done a poo.

😂

"Can I ask you, miss, how many
peeping toms have you cured?"

😆

Fag Ash Lil was a limbo dancer,
she would bend over backwards for anyone.

🤪

I stripped her naked… she'd shaved her fanny,
didn't know which way she was facing.

😃

I used to go out with a Greek porno star
called Linda Lickalotopus.

😂

SUMMERTIME BLUES

Overheard at a nudist camp,
"Is that Dick Brown over there?"

"It sure is, pal, we've had a lovely summer."

Did you know summer was
on a fucking Wednesday last year?

Went on holiday last year, when I opened my case there must have been a hundred pairs of gloves. Our lass said, "Well, you told me just to pack hand luggage." Daft cunt!

At the airport the porter said, "Carry your bag, sir?"

I said, "No thanks, she can walk by her fucking self."

On holiday last year I took my newly bought lilo back to the shop and asked the girl assistant how much she charged for a blowjob.

We always go on holiday in the winter
'cos it's easier to get a deck chair.

Seven days at Butlin's with your girlfriend
makes one week… especially at the knees.

We've sacked the topless waitress…
she was dipping in the till.

When I go on holiday, I always sit at the back of
the plane. Well, you never hear of a plane backing
into a fucking mountain, do you?

Went to Greece on holiday recently, stayed at the
Vagina Hotel. What a hole that turned out to be.
Had a lovely thatched roof though and a very
nice back entrance. They gave us a womb with a
view. Strange thing though, it closes for a full week
once a month while the decorators are in.

OUR LASS

Our lass said she's sick of our new puppy scratching her leather.

I said, "It's your own fault, you shouldn't let him anywhere near your fucking face."

😂

Said to the wife this morning, "I had another dream about you last night. Didn't know you were like that… dirty bastard."

😆

Our house has got subsidence…
still, the wife always wanted a mobile home.

😜

Our lass said she forgot to take her laxative last night.

I said, "No shit!"

😃

Our lass said she was going to buy a leg of lamb for tea last night. So I got a bit of a surprise when I only got a scatty little piece of lamb on my plate. She said, "The leg of lamb was too expensive, I only had enough for a big toe."

Fifty pence for a bunk up.

Our lass said, "What's a bunk up?"

I said, "Fifty pence."

Our lass says she's got something that makes her squirm with delight, but I just can't seem to put my finger on it.

My wife was playing with our puppy. He was pulling at one end of his toy and she was pulling at the other. "Eee," she said, "he does like a good tug first thing on a morning."

I said, "We all do, pet, we all do."

The wife has three endowment policies on me…
always said I was well endowed.

😜

Our lass was doing a crossword.
The clue was 'Adult Insect'. She put daddy.

I said, "Why the fuck daddy?"

She said, "Have you not heard of a daddy long legs?"

😃

Our lass said to me, "Are you losing weight?"

I said, "No I aren't."

She said, "Thought you weren't, fat cunt."

😆

Wife's not clever on her feet… mind you,
she can still count to ten on them.

😂

We've just had the annual scarecrow event in
our village. Residents are asked to make a scarecrow
and put it in their front garden. The wife won it last
year and I wouldn't care, she'd only sat in the front
garden to top up her tan.

MY WIFES GOT SOME PUSSY ON HER

Our lass thinks I've got an obsession with the National Lottery. She said she's sick of hearing me say, "Let's release those big money balls," every time I take my Y-Fronts off.

"Dad, why does mam stay out all night?"

"Shut up, son, and finish your caviar."

We have such a big family that the wife has had to have her ears pierced so the kids can see the telly.

Whenever I bump into my ex-wife there's still a spark. Mind you, I have tried to set her on fire three times.

We've always had a very physical relationship and the wife said, "When I'm on my death bed, will you make love to me one more time?"

So now I've had to promise to back scuttle her through the Pearly Gates.

My fat wife said, "I could eat an apple."

I said, "Don't you mean a fucking orchard."

Wife won the lottery.
She said, "There'll be no sex this weekend."

I said, "It's not a roll-over, then."

She said, "Guess what I've got between
my tits and fanny."

I said, "Most people call it a waist."

I asked her father for her hand in marriage.

He said, "What are your intentions?"

I said, "To fuck her."

Me and our lass were lying in bed this morning
and I said, "Give me a left-handed wank."

She said, "Why left-handed?"

I said, 'Because it feels like someone else's doing it."

MR. ALLCOCK & MR. BROWN

"I say, Mr. Brown, your dog's been chasing people in cars."

"Fuck off Mr. Allcock, he can't have been. He hasn't even got a license."

"Have you been having singing lessons, Mr. Brown?"

"No, I haven't, Mr. Allcock."

"Thought you hadn't, Mr. Brown."

"Cheeky twat, Mr. Allcock."

"I see you're carrying a tailgate, Mr. Brown, where did you get it?"

"It fell off the back of a lorry, Mr. Allcock, not that it's any of your fucking business."

"Did you hear that forty people had died in Thailand, Mr. Brown?"

"What happened, Mr. Allcock, did a fucking bed collapse?"

MY OLD MATE

He's been married six times.
He's not sex mad, just likes wedding cake.

He could get a part in the musical 'Hair',
playing the part of Dan Druff.

My mate owns a clock shop. When I asked him how
his business was doing, he said, "Ticking over."

My mate's so fucking tight that he turns his
windscreen wipers off when he goes under a bridge.

He switches the gas off while
he turns the fucking bacon over.

The tight cunt has a fork in the sugar bowl instead of a spoon.

Me and my best mate used to be champion limbo dancers… yes, we go back a long way.

He was a tightrope walker…
one night he was tight but the rope wasn't.

"A dead fly won't hurt you, mate."

He said, "I know it won't but there's fifty thousand of the little bastards come for the funeral."

"What kind of dog's that, Chubby?"

"Not sure, mate, but last night me dad tripped over it and called it a flat-nosed, hissing basset."

My mate's a chicken farmer. He was really pissed off the other day because somebody had run over his cock.

He's so small that he broke a leg when he fell off the kerb and his parachute never opened.

He's so small he has a downstairs window cleaning round.

He's small and his girlfriend's six foot… poor lad has to jack it in.

His legs are so short that his feet only just reach the floor.

FOOTBALL CRAZY

Me dad took me to my first football match when I was about five years old. I sat on his shoulders as we made our way to the bus stop, my hands sticking tightly to the cap on top of his head because it was covered in tar and oil from his job at the steel works. His cap, not his head, yer daft buggers. Every time I raised my hands his cap came off exposing his bald head, which surprised me somewhat because I'd always thought dad and his cap were conjoined like Siamese twins, and the only way to separate them would be surgically under anaesthetic. Bet you're thinking, 'quite intelligent for a five year old'… fuck… off!

We got to the bus stop and waited for the tram which would take us as far as North Ormesby, there we would get off and walk past the abattoir, then through the streets and Albert Park – where there wasn't time for me to have a go on the swings – all the way to Ayresome Park to watch Middlesbrough FC. Seemed to take ages, can't remember who they were playing.

When the bus arrived it was already pretty full. Although still languishing in the old second division, the Boro still attracted huge crowds. The bus was mainly full of men around me dad's age, all wearing the same greyish-brown caps and Macs. It looked as if they'd all been ambushed by a herd of cattle before they got on the bus and had a cowpat placed strategically on each of their heads, fucking smelt like it too. These men would have been mostly steel workers, with the majority of them doing shift-work. It was always tricky getting time off from shifts and the Personnel Office, which we now know as HR – Human Resources – had a sign outside the office which read, 'Applications to take the day off to attend granny's funeral must be in no later than two days before the match.'

One of the lads said to his mate, "Colin's brought his kid with him to watch Boro for the first time."

His mate said, "Probably wants to introduce him to disappointment while he's still young enough to get over it."

Only joking, I became a lifelong Boro fan, but it is true that after supporting a team like the Boro for so long, I could very likely now take anything life throws at me. I'm sure it's the same for any long time supporter of their favourite football team.

When we got to the ground, dad paid the man on the turnstile for himself and then lifted me over for free. There were other mucky faced young lads with the arse hanging out of their trousers asking complete strangers, "Can I have a squeeze, mister?" which is not a request you'd encourage your kids to be making to any strangers these days. A squeeze, evidently, was what I'd just had off me dad… a lift over the turnstile or a squeeze through if you could both fit. It meant the kid getting into the match for free, whichever way. Don't think I could manage a fucking squeeze these days though.

We stood right at the front, behind a goal. I couldn't really see much, but when the teams came out there was a deafening roar from the crowd, it took me quite by surprise… nearly shit myself. The game started and not much was going on, the roar that greeted the teams when they came on had developed into more of a series of low-pitched gasps and groans. I didn't really understand what was going on. Like the bored five year old that I was, I looked up to the sky, then down to the floor, I'd turn round to look at all the faces behind me, anywhere but towards the football match being played out in front of me. The air was polluted with fag smoke, not an e-cigarette in sight. Nobody there would have believed it if anyone had told them they'd eventually ditch their Woodies and Senior Service, and be dragging on the end of a strawberry or bubblegum flavoured plastic stick in years to come, probably saying, "What the fuck's plastic?"

"Get a pair of fucking glasses, ref!"… "Bet your mam and dad weren't married, ref!"… didn't quite understand that one. One thing that was certain though was that everything happening on the football field appeared to be the ref's fault… what or whoever the fuck a 'ref' was. Then, out of the blue, when I wasn't expecting it, the loudest roar of all. Apparently Boro had scored a goal. The noise scared the living daylights out of me, and when the furore had died down, dad looked down to see me sat at his feet on the concrete step we'd been standing on, shaking and crying my eyes out. Dad immediately picked me up, gave me a rare fatherly hug and said, "Don't worry son, it doesn't happen that often." How true!

As I said, I became a lifelong Boro fan from that day on, going to matches on a regular basis. I used to really enjoy singing along with the rest of the supporters in an attempt to 'encourage' the team to greater efforts, although most were derogatory and aimed at the opposition. We did have a go at our own 'stars' occasionally though. One of my favourites was after we'd bought George Kinnell from Sunderland for a massive £40,000.

It went a bit like this to the tune of 'She'll be coming round the mountain when she comes'…

♪ Oh we paid forty thousand for Kinnell,
Oh we paid forty thousand for Kinnell.
Oh we paid forty thousand, paid forty thousand,
Paid forty thousand for Kinnell, FORKIN HELL! ♪

Up The Boro!

HOME SWEET HOME

Hey, our house is spotless. Yeah, my dog, Spot, ran away at the weekend.

There was a thief around our way that was abseiling down walls and into people's bedrooms. The police finally caught him and gave him a suspended sentence.

My old grandad's just bought a new mattress. He said it's always good to have something to fall back on.

My old nan keeps telling people she's got an Asbo. I've told her loads of times, "No, nan, you've got a gazebo."

My family must think I'm dead boring… when I go to visit my elderly relatives, the first thing they do is take out their hearing aids.

My old grandad's best friend has just died.
Nan said, "Grandad will miss him because
he always said that he was his soul mate."

I said, "No, nan, you misheard him,
he said he was his cell-mate.'

My old uncle's in a home, he's got dementia.
They had a dance night last week and he got a lady up
to dance and said to her, "Do I come here often?"

My sister went on Match.com to find a date.
They try to find someone with similar jobs and
interests. She's a lollipop lady so they fixed her up
with an ice cream man.

My old nan and grandad have replaced their
lawn with Astroturf. They don't believe in letting
the grass grow under their feet.

GREASY SPOON

The chicken was so tough it's now working on the door at Stringfellow's.

The problem with being famous is when you're in a restaurant everyone looks at you… impossible to pinch any spoons.

I said to the waiter, "What's this you've served me in the bowl?"

He said, "It's bean soup, sir,"

I said, "It probably has but how long ago was that?"

Went to a seafood restaurant, I ate so much crab it was enough to knock you sideways.

Do you know that in France their
fast food restaurants serve fucking snails?

I live in a seaside town. We have a pier with a restaurant at the end of it. I was in there the other night and asked for the seafood soup. The waitress said it was off. I said, "Why?"

She said, "The tide's out."

When we give our grandson Alphabetti Spaghetti, he gets really hyper. I think it must be full of eee's.

Me and the wife both wake up gagging in the morning… me for sex, and her for a cup of tea.

This morning, I sat in the garden and had two slices of toast with nothing on. The wife said, "Put some clothes on, the neighbours can see over the fence."

SEX CYMBAL
(WELL I WAS A DRUMMER)

I got my sex education from watching dogs.
For years I went round smelling women's arses.

She was so ugly she was covered
in self-inflicted love bites.

I have a desire to return to the womb… anybody's.

During lovemaking, I shoved her diaphragm up
so far she's wearing it as a shower cap.

Great news, lads… there's a new birth pill
out that changes your DNA.

I knew nothing about sex.
Whenever I got a hard on, me mam used
to tell me it was somewhere to hang your cap.

😃

I'm so unlucky with women that when I rang
a porn line she just said, "Leave me alone."

😅

Some men prefer the right leg, some prefer the left leg
but I like something in between.

😉

I put her on a pedestal so I could see her fanny.

I'm so unlucky… if I was trapped in a room with forty wet pussies, I'd have been born with no tongue.

She went into labour for six hours. Would you believe I was faithful for the whole of that time?

My cock's so big that I had to have my vasectomy done by B&Q.

I haven't had sex for so long I could fuck a scabby horse.

We're now being told to make sure everything we scoff is well cooked, but most of the things I like to munch on are pink in the middle anyway.

IT'S A DOG'S LIFE

The difference between a cat and a dog is that if you call a dog he'll come to you, whereas if you call a cat it will just tell you to fuck off.

Oh, I am sorry, I've gone and got my leg caught in your dog's mouth.

He was done up like a dog's dinner. Mind you, have you seen a fucking dog's dinner?

Came home the other day and my little puppy had eaten a large hole in the living room carpet. When he went for a shit, it came out with a matt finish.

Why can't dogs dance?
Because they've got two left feet.

The only one who doesn't wake up with
dog breath in our house is the fucking dog.

😃

I'd just got out of the shower when my small dog walked in, I said, "Hello, little fella."

The wife said, "Are you talking to your fucking willy again?"

🤣

Police came round our house…
said my dog had been caught on CCTV
doing a shit and run.

🤪

When a dog licks its bollocks, it's the same as when a bloke has a wank. You can tell by the expression on his face and the fag hanging out of its mouth.

😆

My mate was at my house when my dog rolled onto the floor and started licking his own bollocks.

My mate said, "Bloody he'll, I wish I could do that."

So I said, "Throw him a crisp and he might let you."

GRUB UP

Went to the butchers, said,
"Can I have a pig's nose and leave the legs on?"

The girlfriend said to me, "It must be the apple a day that keeps that smile on your face."

I said, "No dear, it's the pear on your chest."

I've tried those meals on wheels, but fuck me, they just keep rolling away from me.

We don't do sex much in our house. The only time our lass gets exited these days is if she's stuffing her face with a cream doughnut. If my prick was a chocolate éclair, I'd be getting blowjobs all fucking day long.

If you are ever caught by Cannibals argue like fuck with them. Cannibals never eat anything that doesn't agree with them.

"Yes sir, I do know tongue comes from an animal's mouth and where a hen's egg comes from, but I assure you, sir, the 'Cock-a-Leaky' soup came out of a tin."

"Waiter, what's this fucking fly doing in my soup?"

"Think it's the breaststroke, sir."

I said to the wife, "We keep getting a load of shit from the Chinese 'cos you always order a number two."

You can get anything knocked off these days. There's a lad in our pub selling illegal shredded meat. The police took him in and he's up at court for pushing pulled pork.

THE FAIRER SEX

Girls don't like you when you've got nits,
especially in your pubes.

All you girls who bought your husbands
video cameras for Xmas must know that
you're going to have to get your fanny out.

Match.com… man with left leg would like to meet
woman with right leg… object to lean on each other.

My sister must be a magician… every boyfriend
she's had just disappears, never to be seen again.

The girls used to call me Bear Grylls because
I was always looking for something juicy
to munch on in the bush.

I once took a girl home that was so ugly
my dick shot up my own arse.

😂

They say black makes you look thin,
that's why obese girls go out with West Indians.

😜

Do you know, she wouldn't hurt a fly unless
it had a willy hanging out of it.

😆

I was going to bring you some flowers
but the cemetery gates were closed.

😃

I've always wanted to be a world
famous mountain climber but I think
I must have peaked too soon.
All the girls used to say that
I peaked too fucking soon.

😂

TECHNOPHOBIA

Everyone I know complains about their Sat Nav.
I'd be fucking lost without mine.

😀

I got a watch with a lifetime guarantee.
When it breaks down a razor comes out
and slashes your fucking wrist.

😆

"Excuse me, can I use your Dictaphone?"
"No. Use your finger like everyone else."

😂

"I like your watch, fatty."
"Yes, I got it on tick."

😉

'Penny for the Guy' went contactless
this year where I live.

😀

Had this watch for years. Still can't get the fucking balls into Mickey Mouse's ears.

"Is that watch gold?"

"It better be or the bloke on the market's done me out of a fucking quid."

Wife bought me a camcorder for Xmas. I took some film but when I played it back we all looked short and fat, so I tried to alter the settings to make us look normal. Then I realised we actually are all short and fat.

At the airport for our last holiday, the wife was getting real excited. She said, "I'm buzzing."

I said, "You must have left your Rampant Rabbit on then."

OUR LASS

Wife said, "There's a mouse in
the food cupboard, dear."

"Just close the door on it, it'll fucking starve to death."

😃

She said she'd take me to the Waldorf,
but when we got there it was just a bit of land
that had been walled off.

😂

When me and our lass have a shag it's
like our belly buttons are having a fight.
Our lass calls it Naval Warfare.

😜

Our lass said, "I'm sick of buying lipstick so often,
I seem to go through it so quickly."

I said, "It's your own fault, you shouldn't have
such a fucking big mouth."

😆

Our lass's doctor has told her she has an irritable bowel. He can't be much of a doctor if he thinks it's only her fucking bowel that's irritable.

"Sorry I'm late, love. Is my dinner still warm?"

She said, "It will be if the bin's on fire."

I said, "There's a funeral over there. I wonder who's dead."

The wife said, "I think it's the one in the box."

Our lass went out and left me babysitting. When she came back she said, "That's not my baby."

I said, "Make your mind up, when you went out you told me to change it."

She treats me like dirt… she hides me under the bed.

Bought the wife a rocket... she's over the moon.

She is such a bad cook, the oven had ulcers.

I had a wet dream last night, our lass was in it.
What a fucking waste of a good wet dream.

She's got me eating out of her hand,
she says it saves on the washing up.

The wife's so worried about getting too fat
that she's gone to see a shrink.

I cuddled up to the back of the wife in bed
this morning and said, "What would you rather
have, pet... a cup of tea or mind blowing,
neverending rampant sex?'

She just said, "Two sugars, please."

Wife came in all flustered and said,
"There's water in the carburettor, darling."

I said, "That's nothing to worry about, pet.
Where's the car?"

"At the bottom of the river."

The wife said to me, "I can't do this jigsaw. Chubby.
I think it's the hardest one I've ever tried to do."

I said, "Put the cornflakes back in the box, pet,
and go and get yourself a new pair of glasses."

The wife says that sex is always better on holiday…
she told me in a text from Benidorm.

We don't lead a very exciting life. These days the wife
thinks living dangerously is getting in the shower
without the anti-slip mat down.

POLICE FARCE

The judge said to me, "I remember you, Mr. Brown. You were up in front of me three years ago for the same offence, stealing an overcoat."

I said, "How long do you think an overcoat lasts?"

I said, "Listen, officer, I've just performed at a policeman's ball, and you know what policeman's balls are like. They brought the audience in with blankets over their heads."

I was stopped by a police car and the police officer came over and said, "I've stopped you because one of your rear lights appears to be not working, sir."

I said, "It's done that before," and got out of the car, went to the back, kicked the light and it came straight back on.

The police officer said, "Very good, sir, and now perhaps you might like to go round the front and kick your tax disc to see if that comes up to date too.'

We had a policeman at our front door yesterday.
He said, "Chubby, why did you hit your
lass with a chair?"

I said, "Because I couldn't lift the fucking sideboard."

The judge said, "Is this the first time
you've been up before me?"

I said, "I don't know, what time do you get up?"

One night I was driving and a copper pulled me over,
he said, "Would you mind blowing into this, sir?"

I said, "What is it?"

He said, "It's a bag and it tells you if
you've had too much to drink."

I said, "Oh, I've got one of them at home…
the wife."

He said, "You were driving erratically all over the road, didn't you see the arrows?"

I said, "I didn't even see the fucking Indians."

😆

He said, "I've reason to believe that you're drunk and you shouldn't be driving."

I said, "You don't expect me to walk home in this state, do you?"

😃

Why are you coming home at three o'clock in the morning?

The police raided the party.

😂

Where do policemen live?

Let's be Avenue.

😜

RANDOM

When I was a kid I used to watch a TV programme called 'Junior Criss Cross Quiz', it was a quiz show for kids. At the end of each show the presenter would ask a question for the young viewers and invite us all to send the answer in. He said, "All of the correct answers will be placed in a container and one will be pulled out at random." Well, for years I thought Random was somewhere near Leeds. I know what you're thinking… 'Daft cunt!'

Anyway, this section is a collection of jokes out of the blue, from thin air, and off the top of my fucking head, all of which have been pulled out at Random, somewhere near Leeds.

"Excuse me, sir, did you knock me down with your car the other day?"

"What makes you think it was me?"

"Oh, I recognised the laugh."

That Steve Redgrave is always sticking
his fucking oar in.

😆

These NHS cuts are getting worse.
The other night I turned the telly on to watch
Casualty and was left sitting there for three hours
until the bastard thing came on.

😃

Little girl on the bus with a bag of toffees.
I said, "You've a hair on your sweetie, pet."

She said, "I know and I'm only fourteen."

😂

He was such a good salesman,
he could have sold a double bed to the Pope.

😜

We call our dog Minge, because he's hairy and smells
a lot… he also has a drip on the end of his nose.
Our lass got rid of him 'cos she was sick of lads
asking if they could stroke her minge.

😂

Pulled into the petrol station and the girl attendant came out. I said, "Fifty pence worth of petrol, please."

She said, "Would you like me to sneeze into your tyres while I'm at it, sir?" … cheeky mare.

After sex, I said, "Were you faking it?"

She said, "No, I really was asleep."

Since the new smoking laws came in, mice testing cigarettes now have to stand outside the cage.

"My dog's got no nose."

"Well how does it smell then?"

"Fucking awful."

The man who wrote 'The Hokey Cokey' died. What a fucking job they had getting him in the coffin.

MR. ALLCOCK & MR. BROWN

"Did you know Mr. Brown, they are now saying that if you drink 12 cups of water a day you can expect to live an extra 4 years."

"Interesting, Mr. Allcock, but you'll probably spend most of your extra 4 years on the fucking loo."

"I say, Mr. Brown, I have some photographs of you and my wife sharing a bath. What have you got to say for yourself?"

"Oh, I'll have two of those and one of those, thank you very much Mr. Allcock."

"I hear your brother's coming from America, Mr. Brown. How will you recognise him after 25 years?"

"I won't have to, Mr. Allcock. He'll recognise me 'cos I haven't fucking been away."

"Mr. Brown, give me a four letter word regularly used in a brothel."

"That's an easy one, Mr. Allcock… next."

THINGS I CAN'T STAND

The phone rings when you're halfway through a wank.

Wives who ask for money
then tell you they're on a period.

People who sing,
♫ 'When Elaine is in my ears and in my eyes' ♫
to the tune of Penny Lane… daft cunts.

Liars who say people live happily ever after.

Fucking fanny farts.

MY OLD FLAMES (DIRTY BITCHES)

She was so thick she had to take
her bra off to count to two.

She was so thin that she had a tattoo on her chest,
'In case of rape, this side up.'

She always sings when she takes a bath…
you can hear her every January, July and August.

Match.com… man with kite wishes
to meet lady with wind.

After my divorce and before I got married again,
I went a bit bonkers, getting up to all sorts of
daft things… I think I was having a mid-wife crisis.

I'm a diver and my name's muff... I'm a muff-diver.

Are you on your own? Been a good girl?
That's why you're on your own.

I was chatting a girl up the other night.
She was obviously an animal lover because when
I asked her if she wanted to go out the next night,
she said she was having a night in with her rabbit.

My ex-wife would go out with any Tom or Harry...
never was one for Dick though.

She had shoes from Italy, dress from Paris,
handbag from London and a belly from Greggs.

She was so thick she thought a Vindaloo
was a toilet in an Italian wine bar.

She's had four husbands, all cremated…
she's got husbands to burn.

😂

She said, "I don't like the look of that fish."
Have you ever seen a good-looking fish?

😜

Where did you get your face? The Argos catalogue?

😃

Stop looking around, let's face it Brad Pitt
will never fuck you but, then again, I might.

😆

I said, "What's the use of pulling your knickers up
if they're crotchless?"

😂

I can remember when I used to climax
and splash a girl on the underside of her chin.
Now it only happens if I get a soapy tit wank.

😂

She was young enough to be Woody Allen's next wife.

I can't concentrate on oral sex with her mother's face
pressed up against the window.

She was so fat that she had to pull
her knickers down to scratch her nipples.

She was eating for two… she had a tape worm.

I ran a bath for her but before she got in
I had to grease the sides.

I said, "Why is there a tyre lever on the bed?"

She said, "I was putting my thong on."

HEARD IT DOWN THE PUB

Took this girl for a game of golf,
got a hole in one and a feel in the other.

Never told anyone I wore a wig…
liked to keep it under my hat.

He believed in re-incarnation
so he left all his money to himself.

If I get re-incarnated, I'd like to
come back as a lady's bicycle seat.

Back in the sixties they used to separate
the boys from the men with a crowbar.

CHUBBY AT THE BAR

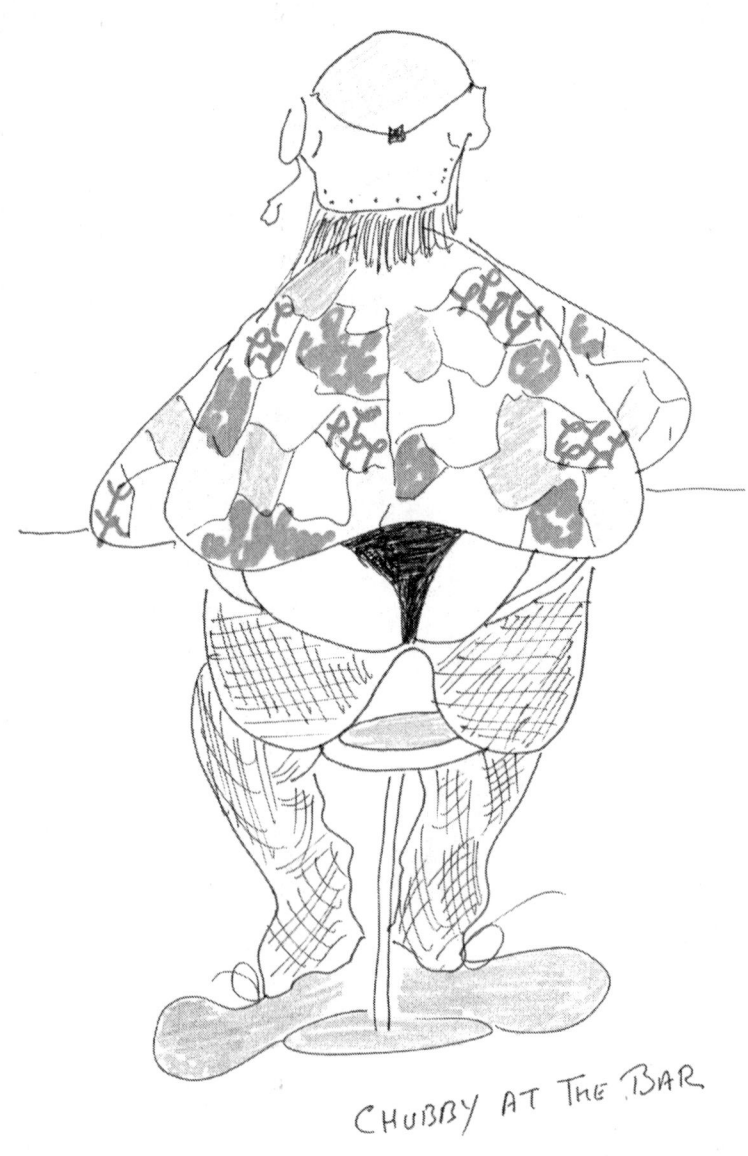

I answered the telephone.

"Is that you, Chubby?"

"Yes it is."

The voice came back and said,
"Can you lend me fifty quid?"

I said, "Hang on, it's a bad line, I can't quite hear you."

The operator said, "I can hear him alright."

I said, "Well you lend him fifty fucking quid then."

Nosey bastard.

😂

The old sea captain was deaf
'cos he had no Buccaneers.

😉

It was the local Agoraphobic's Annual General
Meeting last week. Same as usual, no one turned up.

😃

I went to the bar and I said, "Mine's a light."

The barman said, "Well throw a
bucket of water over it."

😆

DOCTOR I'M IN TROUBLE

"Doctor I'm suffering from kleptomania."

"Have you taken anything for it?"

A man said to the doctor, "I think I've got AIDS."

Doctor said, "Go home, take some sennapods and have a big bowl of prunes, then treat yourself to a large bar of chocolate laxative."

The man said, "Will that cure me, doctor?"

Doctor said, "No, but it will show you what your arse is really for."

Fellow says to the doctor, "Please help me out, me and my wife have no sex life at all."

Doctor said, "Why don't you try it like animals? Most animals have a great sex life, especially cats."

The very next day the doctor bumped into the man in the street carrying a large bunch of flowers.

He said, "I'm going to the hospital to see the wife. I took your advice but while we were shagging, she fell off the shed roof."

I said to the doctor, "I can't stop stealing things."

The doctor said, "Take these tablets and if they don't work get me a colour telly."

The man in the hospital bed said, "Nurse, give me a kiss."

She said, "No I can't."

He said, "Go on, I won't put my tongue in your mouth."

She said, "No!"

He said, "Well just let me feel your tits then."

She said, "For the last time… no! I shouldn't even be giving you a blowjob really."

Doctor said, "You need to lose some weight, Mr. Brown. Stop booking a meal for four and then going on your own."

ATTILA THE MOTHER-IN-LAW

Mother-in-law walked in and the budgie
threw himself into the cat's mouth.

She's more frightening than
Hannibal Lector's fucking cookbook.

She's that fat and ugly, even her imaginary friend
won't be seen out with her.

She's that useless, she couldn't find an
Eskimo with diarrhoea on a bike.

I wouldn't say the mother-in-law was fat but
she's started hiring herself out as a bouncy castle.

She hates me so fucking much that if a
swarm of bees attacked me in the garden,
she'd run out and cover me with honey.

😃

She reckons she can walk on water but
she does have webbed fucking feet.

😝

I've just heard your mother has come off her
motorbike. I told you she should never have
taken that job on the wall of death.

😆

The mother-in-law's got three weeks to live…
don't worry, it'll soon pass.

😂

The mother-in-law looks like a million dollars.
Have you ever seen a million dollars?
It's green, wrinkled and weighs a ton.

😃

We have a photo of the mother-in-law pinned to our gate to keep the fucking dogs away from the garden.

You will recognise the mother-in-law…
her photo is on every pirate's flag.

I bought her a crocodile handbag…
hope it bites her fucking hand off.

She got a splinter in her finger
after scratching her head.

She's a greedy bastard… if she had to wear a patch,
it would be of barbecue sauce.

The other day the mother-in-law was a bag of nerves,
which is unusual 'cos usually she's just a fucking bag.

Mother-in-law came round so I whacked her with the shovel again.

She's an alcoholic… gets a catalogue from Oddbins every month.

When she fell on the floor her skirt blew up and I could see her fanny. There are only two things that fuck old women… hypothermia and me.

She's so ugly… if a wasp stung her, he'd close his eyes.

She's so fat, her blood type is BLT.

The mother-in-law got kidnapped last year. The kidnappers sent me a letter demanding £50,000 or they'd send her back.

LITTLE OLD ME

She said, "Rome wasn't built in a day, Chubby."

I said, "Well I wasn't on that job."

Some people can't control when they laugh, they often laugh in the wrong places. In fact, some people even laugh at funerals. I know I did at the ex-wife's, because it meant I didn't have to pay her any more fucking maintenance.

When I was teenager, we had a pawn shop near us that sold mucky books. You could take in some of your old rubbish you wanted get rid of and swap it for a mucky book. We used to call it 'Tit for Tat.'

No, it wasn't much fun being a young fat lad… none of my mates would play on the fucking see-saw with me.

You know I'm so unlucky with love that my blow-up doll stood me up the other night. She was probably just getting her own back for the other week when I let her down.

I once paid for six prostitutes but could only manage three. One of them said, "Your fucking eyes are bigger than your bell-end, mate."

They say you can laugh a girl into bed. I don't know about that but I've certainly laughed a few out of bed.

I worked in a karate school… the wages were shit but I got plenty of backhanders.

I felt a bit deflated the day after my birthday when I realised it would be another 364 days before the family had to be nice to me again.

BRASS MONKEYS

You know it was so foggy this morning that when
I got out of my car to get something from the boot,
I couldn't find my way back to the driver's door.

It was so cold last night, I fell out of bed
this morning and snapped my pyjamas.

When I woke up this morning there
was a two inch cube of ice in my bed.
I took it out and stood it on the radiator.
Five minutes later it went faaaaarrrrtt.
(You'll have to do the noise yourself)

It was so cold that when I threw some bread
out for the birds, they just sat on it.

It was that cold I saw a dog with ear-muffs on.

The storm was so bad I spotted
Siamese twins looking for each other.

I saw an old lady the other day wearing just one glove. I asked her why she was only wearing the one glove, and she said that just before she came out she'd been watching the weather forecast, and the chap on there said it was going to be warm, but on the other hand it might be cold.

I had to snap my dog off a lamp post this morning.

I was driving over the moors one foggy night…
it was so foggy that you couldn't see your hand
in front of you, when suddenly a red light
appeared in the distance. It got clearer and clearer,
turned out to be the end of my cigarette.

MAM & DAD

As I said earlier, mam and dad fought like cat and dog, eventually divorcing when I was about ten and divorce wasn't fashionable then. My dad used to say, "Coming home to a kiss and a cuddle, coming home to love and affection, coming home to your tea on the table meant you'd come home to the wrong bastard house."

Dad wasn't what you would call a romantic. Most blokes weren't in those days. I think the most romantic thing I ever saw him do was bring me mam a small bottle of Cherry B home from the club one Xmas Eve after he'd been pissing it up all night with his mates. He said to me mam one night, after she'd been harping on about wanting to go out, "Do you want to go out? Do you really want to go out?" He often said things twice.

She said, "Yes I do."

He said, "Well, go and get a shovel of coal, then."

We had a coal fire then and the coal bunker was at the bottom of the yard, next to the outside toilet.

I think me mam and dad met at the local cinema. Mam was an usherette. Dad used to say that she held a torch for him, and mam used to say that the batteries must have been dud then. As well as being an usherette, she sold the ice creams during the interval. When it came to getting married, me mam walked backwards up the aisle in the church.

Dad Alas at the door he said he looks like me

There wasn't much money around and mam used to economise by making me wear hand-me-downs off me dad. His trousers gave me the most trouble, when I had to undo the zip fly just to blow my fucking nose. She'd get the rest of our clothes from the local Army and Navy surplus clothes shop. I must admit I felt like a right idiot going to school dressed as a Japanese General.

It was getting near Xmas one year, and I had to go past the pawnbrokers on my way to school. There was a bike in the window; I'd always wanted a bike so I'd stand there for a few minutes every morning with my nose pressed up against the steamy window, dreaming that this bike could be mine one day. I built up the courage to mention it to me dad, hoping he might buy it and surprise me on Xmas morning. I said, "Dad, dad," saying things twice was catching, "I've got me eye on a bike."

He came back as quick as a flash, "Well keep your eye on it, son, 'cos you aren't getting your fucking arse on it." Even after that, if re-incarnation turns out to be true, I'd still like to come back as a ladies bicycle seat.

Dad had a war record... it was Vera Lynn singing 'We'll Meet Again.' Actually he fought with Montgomery in North Africa and Mountbatten in Burma. Couldn't get on with no fucker, me dad. Dad was a strong union man, if he ever told us bedtime stories he would always start off with 'once upon a time and a half.' Although he worked at the steel works throughout his life he'd never been able to hold down a job for very long, but at one stage he had nine hundred men below him… he used to cut the grass at the local cemetery. He used to bring me mam a bunch of flowers home every Friday. She never knew why she stopped getting them when he got fired from the cemetery. He worked in a bank for a while and got caught pinching a pen. Ended up in prison, just like the rest of the family, where he decided to dig a tunnel to escape. Some feat that was, it took him six months, thing was he'd only been given three.

The truth is that there was nothing mam wouldn't do for me dad, and there was nothing dad wouldn't do for me mam. In fact, that's exactly how they got through their married life… doing fuck all for each other.

POLICE FARCE

I got pulled up by the police while I was driving. I was trying to act all sober but he kept going on. The wife leaned over me and said to him, "I'd calm down if I were you, he can get into a right temper after he's had a good drink."

Mate said, "There's a Black Maria outside."

I said, "Let her in, there's no discrimination in this house."

I was walking home at midnight, when I was stopped by a policeman. He said there had been some robberies in the area that night. I said I'd been at my girlfriend's all night. He said could I prove it. So I gave him my fingers to smell. He let me go.

I've got a zip on the side of my trousers and
I was arrested when I went for looking for change.

He's such a twat… if it wasn't for him
the police would be out of work.

Police wanted to know his movements
but he's so lazy he doesn't have any.

He's a maniac-klepto… walks backwards into shops
and leaves things.

Read in the paper today that someone has stolen
a van carrying Viagra tablets. Police say they
are looking for a hardened criminal and when
they catch him, he'll get a stiff sentence.

A cricket player has been arrested for stabbing an opponent with a cricket stump. Police have bailed him.

I was taken to court… the charge was assault with a friendly weapon.

An old dear dialled 999, said that her house was absolutely full of spiders, flies, wasps and other insects… the police sent the SWAT team in.

The local post office has been robbed by a six-foot robber and a five-foot robber… the police are looking high and low for them.

I got pulled up driving by the police; the officer said, "Okay, Lewis Hamilton, you were doing fifty miles per hour in a thirty limit. What's your hurry?"

I said, "Sorry officer, but I'm late for my speed awareness course."

OUR LASS

We had an Elvis wedding, got married to
'Burning Love'… wish I'd set her alight
there and then.

Wife said, "I've got an awful pain right
in between my shoulder blades,
I don't know where it's coming from."
I said, "I've just stabbed you, daft get."

Wife was eating porridge this morning and some
had trickled out of her mouth and down her chin.
Rather reminded me of the DVD I'd stayed up late
to watch the night before.

Our lass is so tight, she's started to mark the fucking
toilet roll to make sure I don't use too much paper.

I said to the wife, "It might be dry enough to do the lawn today."

She said, "What, cut it?"

I said, "No, give it a fucking curly perm. What do you think?"

😃

I said to the wife, "Where's the fireside chair, pet?"

She said, "I've sold it, you told me yesterday that I was sitting on a fortune."

😂

"Do you like my dress, pet?"

"It looked better when it was still full of potatoes."

🤪

The wife goes to keep fat classes.

😂

Our lass said, "I've seen your willy on the menu at KFC…a mini chicken dipper… ha ha.!"

I said, "Yeah well, I do put it into your boneless bucket every night."

I've just got rid of twelve stone of ugly fat…
divorced the wife.

The kids call their mam Doorbell
'cos she's got no knockers.

"Is that your lass, Chubby?"

"'Course it is, you don't think
I'd be shacking up with her, do you?"

Trying to lose weight, the wife bought
a slimming magazine, but she ate it.

I said to the wife, "The clocks go back next week."

She said, "Well you should have
kept up the payments."

My wife's quite emotional. Every time I ask her to give me a blowjob she says she gets a lump in her throat.

We were going out and the wife said,
"I haven't got time for a shower, I'm just going to do the three 'Fs', face, feet and fanny."

I said, "I'm just going to do the three 'Fs' too, face, feet, and fucking big willy."

😆

The wife only lets me shag her when she wants something... like timing a boiled egg... soft boiled, of course.

😂

When me and the wife sleep together it's a bit like Morecambe and Wise... there's only one funny one, nothing ever happens, and she's got short fat hairy legs.

😀

Our lass is dead dozy sometimes. Only this morning, she said, "You know when I wake up, my eyelids are still stuck together?"

I said, 'Well, you haven't fucking woke up then have you, daft cunt."

I came in and caught the wife dyeing her minge.
I said, "What are you doing that for?"

She said, "It makes my fanny look younger."

I said, "Well try dyeing your fucking face then."

Our lass caught me shagging her mate up the arse,
she cried out, "You can't do that to me."

I said, "Exactly! That's why I'm doing it to your mate."

Me and the wife were on holiday and she decided to put her feet in one of those tanks where the fish nibble your feet. I said, "What do you want to do that for?"

She said, "It's good for you, the fish eat away at any imperfections you might have on your feet."

I said, "Can't you get your fucking head in it?"

SEX CYMBAL (WELL I WAS A DRUMMER)

Men name their penises tool, weapon, cock,
John Thomas, and Percy... I call mine a mouthful.

There's a new perfume out called 'Nothing'.
I asked my girlfriend if she would wear it
and got a slap in the face.

They called her Dandelion
'cos she kept pissing the bed.

My girlfriend's a bit like a wardrobe...
tall with drawers.

I still have a healthy sex life, but,
whatever you do, don't tell the wife.

"Would you like to sit down, pet?"

"No thanks," she said, "I've just come back from my honeymoon."

😃

She made crepe suzette with crepe bandages… tasted fucking crepe as well.

😂

Your skin is like a peach… ever seen a 25 year old peach?

😜

You know it's true love when you start having wet dreams about your girlfriend instead of her sister.

😆

I once had a girlfriend called Annette, and when we were doing it 'doggy style', I couldn't resist punching the air and shouting, "Back of Annette."

But I'm married now and when me and our lass have our leg-over, I say, "It's in the bag."

Dont know what women see in you

I went to the sperm bank the other day.
I said, "How do you make a deposit?"

The girl said, "You have to use the hole in the wall."

I've been knocking off the girl next door. The other
night I came home from work and she was waving
through her window for me to go in and see her.
I knew my tea was waiting for me at home, so it was
a straight choice of 'Toad in the Hole' or just Hole…
so I thought, 'Fuck the toad.'

I love tall girls… they lie longer in bed.

A girl I once went out with was kissing
my bare chest. She pulled a face and said,
"What's that on your chest? It tastes awful."

I said, "I sprayed deodorant on it
to make it smell nice."

She said, "Well, it tastes fucking awful."

I said, "There's none on my willy."

MR. ALLCOCK & MR. BROWN

"How did you meet the wife, Mr. Brown."

"Quite easily, Mr. Allcock, I just opened my wallet and she was there like a flash."

"You know, Mr. Allcock, my wife always reminds me of cheese."

"What do you mean, Mr. Brown. Like Dutch Edam… smooth and mysterious, or Danish Blue… dark and dangerous, or maybe Mature Cheddar… strong and tasty?"

"No, Mr. Allcock, like fucking Laughing Cow."

"I say, Mr. Brown, I rang your phone yesterday but it was dead."

"Yes it was, Mr. Allcock. I was at a funeral."

"Have you noticed, Mr. Brown, there's a pygmy
and a dwarf behind the bar?"

"Yes I have, Mr. Allcock, the landlord told me he was
cutting down on staff. He's also employed a midget
waitress to make the meal portions look bigger."

"I've got a confession to make, Mr. Brown,
I've been going into brothels."

"I find that rather strange, Mr. Allcock,
I thought you didn't like soup."

"The wife's always tried to keep her body in shape,
Mr. Brown, but when you get to a certain age
it all goes tits up."

"Don't you mean tits down, Mr. Allcock?"

THERE'S A BLOKE GETS IN OUR PUB...

He has the IQ of a piece of fucking dried bread.

What a fucking liar, he says he's a long distance lorry driver on The Isle of Man.

He's been drinking Domestos, no wonder he's clean round the bend.

He's so small he hires himself out to stand on top of wedding cakes.

Greedy cunt … he won a holiday for two and went twice on his own

His imaginary friend wouldn't speak to him.

He found a crutch so he went home
and broke his own fucking leg.

He says that anyone who puts money
away for their own burial are just digging
a fucking big hole for themselves.

He broke into Ladbrokes…
by the time the police arrived
he'd already lost £250.

He was so tough he had twigs on his chest.

He says he worked in a gold mine,
but then got caught pinching lead off the roof.

The landlord said to him,
"Hey there's no smoking allowed in here."

He said, "I'm not smoking allowed,
I'm smoking quietly."

He's never worked a day in his life…
he's on the council.

There was a fight in the pub so I said to him,
"Did you get hurt in the fracas?"

He said, "No, just a kick in the bollocks."

He had a mole on the end of his dick
so I reported him to the RSPCA.

He's so hard he uses barbed wire
instead of dental floss.

HOME SWEET HOME

My old uncle's been admitted to the local loony bin. He thinks he's a crane. I telephoned to see how he was doing, and they've told me he's picking up.

Two crocodiles were having their leg over on David Attenborough's show on telly, when my young grandson said, "What are they doing, grandad?"

I said, "Making a handbag."

My old nan's got a new dog… she says it's a sack-a-poo. It's cock-a-poo really.

My sister thinks she's accommodating just because she runs a Bed & Breakfast.

I said to my mam, "Mam, where do I come from?"

She said, "Why, you sweet little thing,
you came from the sugar bowl."

I went to my dad and said, "Mam's just told me
I came from the sugar bowl."

Dad said, "Aye, that's about the bloody size of it."

My father was that much of a betting man that
he would even bet on the clothes horse... still lost.

Granddaughter came home with a tattoo.
Well, I went fucking mad with her. Then she said,
"So it's okay for my gran to have tattoos on her legs,
but not me then?"

I said, "They aren't tattoos, they're varicose veins."

We were due to have friends over for tea
so I splashed out and bought a toilet roll.

HEARD IT DOWN THE PUB

Fanny's like having a beer… the older you get,
the less you can manage in one go.

How did you get that hairstyle?
Did you put your fingers in a socket
or go through the carwash on your bike?

Six foot twelve man standing at the door says,
"What you laughing at, fatty?"

I said, "Oh nothing, I'm just giving
my teeth some fresh air."

I wouldn't say the landlord in my local pub
was on the fiddle, but he's even started
diluting the fucking water now.

Jordan's got new shoes, but she doesn't know yet.

The six million dollar man has put
a one-armed bandit up the stick.

A friend of mine stole a hand grenade
and went off without telling his wife…
boom boom!

Seventy-five years old and not one grey hair
on his head… well, he is completely bald.

I have a friend who invites his dates in for a coffee…
from his vending machine.

At the National Blowjob Championships last week,
the winner gave a jaw-dropping performance.

A mate of mine in the pub is a bit of a
nancy-boy, but he likes to think of himself
as a bit of an old rocker. He says his favourite song
is 'A Walk On The Mild Side'.

DOCTOR I'M IN TROUBLE

An apple a day keeps the doctor away
but body odour does the same thing.

I went to the doctors… I said, "Every time I sit down I think that there's another one of me sat next to me… I'm beside myself with worry."

Our lass has always been a bit of an exhibitionist. She was at the doctors for an internal examination. The doctor said, "Would you like a nurse to be present?"

She said, "No thanks but you can bring some of your mates in, if you like."

Hospitals are trying to encourage men to attend ante-natal classes, so they have started to teach expectant fathers how to 'Dad Dance'.

Doctor put me on a stable diet… I have to have my oats twice a day. Well that's what I told our lass.

😂

My shit was such a funny colour that the doctor thought I'd swallowed a box of crayons.

🤪

The ringing in my ears was so bad that I got a fucking telephone bill.

😆

I told my doctor that my bowel movements were as regular as clockwork… 7.30 every morning… the problem is that I don't get up until 8.00.

😃

I was once asked to donate my sperm. I said I'm not going to that fucking sperm bank… it's all a load of wank.

😂

I saw this title on a book the other day, 'Incontinence… read it and wee'.

JACK THE LAD

I hated school like fuck, didn't like the milk they made us drink every morning at ten o'clock. Never forget taking a letter home to dad that said the school meals were going up, and thinking to myself, 'Fuck me, going up? It takes me all the time to keep the fucking slop down.'

I was like an Irish Robin Hood. I used to rob anybody and keep it. One day I recollect a group of neighbours congregated round, muttering to each other, "Well, who would take her purse?"

I said, "Thieving bastards, whoever they are."

I still bought two pounds worth of broken biscuits with the money… always feeding my fucking face. Dad found out and took the skin off my arse, which was the one and only time I've lost weight, even Houdini wouldn't have got out of one of his headlocks.

One of me dad's favourite sayings was, "Stop talking to yourself or they'll lock you away." I used to say that I wasn't talking to myself, it was just that no one else was listening to me. Mam had a saying if I was in trouble, "If I come over there, our Roy, I'll be with you," and if she did, she was… ouch! We were all tearaways then. My mate Nander was so tough he used to bite the fucking police dogs.

I realised I was never going to be a puff when I got

my first look at a real live hairy fanny, it was love at first sight… proper bushes in those days, no one had ever heard of a Brazilian, apart from Pele that is. After that most of my pocket money was spent on mucky books. Spic & Span was my favourite, and I used to think one day I'd be on page three, because the girl on page two had the biggest pair of fucking tits I'd ever seen, so whenever anyone closed the book they'd be right in my face… hoo-la-la. Well, I think you've got the picture.

I became a Teddy Boy before I could grow the statutory side-burns, so I used my sister's mascara pencil to draw them on. They looked fucking great until one night when I took surrender Brenda to the local Lyric cinema to see the new Elvis Presley film hoping to get a bit of back seat action. Surrender was her nickname because she used to give in easily. King Creole was Elvis's new film, but I was hoping to get a bit Crinkly Hole. We were stood outside waiting in the queue for the last house, when it started to pour down. Well, my mascara drawn side-burns began to run so, within minutes, instead of looking like this hard as fuck Teddy boy, I looked more like Chichi the fucking Panda. To add to that, my fucking drainpipe trousers were doing the very job they were designed for too. So there was no Crinkly fucking Hole that night.

MY OLD FLAMES (DIRTY BITCHES)

When she bought a new coat I said,
"I bet you paid through the nose for that."

She said, "No, but you are close."

She's bedridden, but sometimes
she likes it on the carpet.

Every time I look at her face it reminds me
that I don't like scrambled egg.

Her chest was so flat you could play pool on it.

She was so thin that when she sat on the back of
my motorbike she looked like a radio aerial.

We used to call her 'okey cokey'
because she pushed it in, pulled it out
and then shook it all about.

😃

Then I played darts with her… well, her head
did go to a fucking point.

🤪

The girlfriend said to me, "You know,
sometimes our love making can be a
right pain in the arse, especially if you come
to bed without your specs on."

😆

It was so cold she was wearing a balaclava…
ever seen a terrorist in a frock?

😂

She was so old she lost her virginity
to William the Conqueror.

🤪

Her vagina had cobwebs, straw and mice.

She carried a donor card in case
Julius Caesar wanted a kidney.

She was so stupid she bought a
mountain bike in Norfolk.

Bought her an ice cream… I said,
"Do you want hundreds and thousands?"

She said, "No, one will do, thanks."

Blowjob out of the question…
she got lockjaw eating the ice cream.

I had a girlfriend who made animals out of balloons.
After a sixty nine, I was pulling my undies on and
realised she'd twisted my dick into a duck.

THE MOST WONDERFUL TIME OF THE YEAR

I'm not very good with presents. Last year I bought my wife a Cuckoo Clock for Xmas. It didn't work properly so I took it back to the shop. The shop assistant said the fucking cuckoo had agoraphobia.

The wife's put her Xmas list in early this year, she handed it to me the other day…
it said, 'Fuck off, fat cunt.'

The wife had been out shopping and came back with something that she gave to me, she said, "You can wrap that up and give me it for Xmas."

Then she gave me the receipt.

I said, "What's that for?"

She said, "In case I don't like it and you have to take it back."

OUR LASS

I don't watch porn with the wife
'cos I don't want her saying,
"Now that's what I call a cock."

The wife said, "I'm leaving you."
I said, "If you're passing B&Q get me some poles
for the girls who are coming tonight."

I married the wife under the condition
she went around all the gents toilets and
scrubbed her name off the walls.

Our lass came in from shopping and said that she'd
seen my name on the side of a loaf of bread, but
when she got closer she realised it said, 'Thick cut'.

People often refer to the wife as 'the better half'.
Considering I'm twice the fucking size of my missus,
our family refer to her as 'the better third.'

The only thing me and our lass have in common
these days is the size of our tits.

Our lass has been helping the milkman this week…
just till his horse gets better.

The wife tried to gas herself…
she threw herself into the North Sea.

The wife's in rehab and the doctor's said
that if she has one more drink she'll be dead…
so I've thrown her a six-pack over the wall.

She's started buying Jumbo Toilet rolls… exactly how big does she think my fucking arse is?

I said to the wife, "Why don't you moan when we're having sex?"

She said, "There isn't the time."

The wife was up the ladders washing the windows and I couldn't resist taking a peek. I said, "You've got a party popper stuck up your fanny?"

She said, "I have not."

I said, "You have… I can see the string hanging down."

Our lass thinks an erogenous zone is where only the local residents can park their cars.

I said to the wife, "We're dead lucky to have each other you know. There are plenty of people our age who haven't got anyone to have a fucking good argument with."

SEX CYMBAL
(WELL I WAS A DRUMMER)

She was as much use as a clothes brush
in a nudist camp.

I watched her get ready for bed. Max Factor,
Nivea and a mud pack… by the time we got to bed,
I felt like I was being sucked into a bed of quicksand.

She asked me for something with diamonds…
so I bought her a pack of cards.

She slept like a baby… with her big toe in her mouth.

She said, "I got a yankee up yesterday,
and I'm seeing him again tomorrow."

ITs PAST MY
BED TIME CHUBBS YOU'LL
HAVE TO SHAG ME ON THE
SETTEE. OK.

I once worked in a funeral parlour, and the boss let me use the hearse to take a new girlfriend out one night. When I called at her house to pick her up, she wouldn't get in the car, she said she wouldn't be seen dead in it.

"What's that bit on the end of a Durex for?"

"It's for putting your foot on when you're taking it off, big boy."

"How much did you pay for that new bra? Six quid? I'd have held them up for you for half the price."

She had no roof in her mouth… when it rained she nearly drowned.

Mary had a little lamb… the shepherd got fired.

MR. ALLCOCK & MR. BROWN

"I saw an interesting story in the newspaper today, Mr. Brown. Someone has made a rocket out of pastry, filled it with steak and kidney, and then launched it."

"Sounds like pie in the sky to me, Mr. Allcock."

"I say, Mr. Brown, a mate of mine went to see a clairvoyant and she charged him £50."

"Daft bastard, the clairvoyant must have seen him coming, Mr. Allcock."

"I say, Mr. Brown, did you know that 50% of men play with themselves in the shower and the other 50% sing?"

"No, I didn't know that, Mr. Allcock."

"Do you know what they sing, Mr. Brown?"

"No I don't, Mr. Allcock."

"I didn't think you would, Mr. Brown, didn't think you would."

"I went to the doctor's this morning, Mr. Allcock, and asked him if he could give me some more sleeping tablets for the wife?"

"Why did you do that, Mr. Brown? He gave you a big bottle with a hundred in only last week."

"I know he did, Mr. Allcock, but the daft cow's gone and woke up."

"Did I tell you, Mr. Allcock, I'm on a diet?"

"You don't look like you're on a diet, Mr. Brown."

"That's why I'm on a fucking diet, Mr. Allcock."

"Mr. Allcock, my wife bites her own toe nails."

"That's nothing unusual, Mr. Brown, I've heard of quite a few people who are double jointed that bite their own toe nails."

"Not while they're fucking driving, Mr. Allcock, not while they are driving."

NOT SO LITTLE DRUMMER BOY

I think I must have come from a musical background, because I can remember the police knocking on our door at two o'clock one morning and asking me dad if they could see the loot (lute). I didn't take up playing the piano seriously until I was a little older, but I did have one piano lesson when I was in my early teens. My piano teacher was a short, fat, old spinster, whose teeth nearly fell out when I told her I only wanted to learn how to play 'Great Balls of Fire' by Jerry Lee Lewis. I don't think she'd ever heard of him before, and I still don't know what the fuck she thought 'Great Balls of Fire' was all about because she squeaked in a sort of high pitched condescending sort of way, "You'll learn how to play scales just like my other students."

I thought, 'Scales? What the fuck's she on about?' The only scales I knew about were the ones I used to avoid… though I've not always been a fat bastard.

I sat down, couldn't wait to start tinkling with her ovaries… sorry, I mean ivories. I'd only been playing for a few minutes when she said, "Do you know, Roy, I've never seen anyone play the piano quite like you." My face was a picture of sheer glee, but then she followed it by slamming the lid down and breaking two of my bastard toes. I thought, 'Fuck that for a lark,' and didn't go back. In fact, at that point, I thought the piano was definitely not for me.

I used to see the local Boy's Brigade march along Bolckow Road in Grangetown playing their instruments, taking great notice of the little fat lad at the back banging a fucking enormous bass drum. I thought I could do that, but the chances of the local Boy's Brigade letting a reprobate like me join them was about the same as me catching The Pope having a wank. So I started banging away on anything I could get my hands on, bit like I am now really. No, I'd use anything I could find to act as a percussion instrument, that's a drum to the uninitiated. I'd tap away on the armchair at home, and even my school desk, which often ended when my teacher decided to tap away on the back of my fucking head. If it didn't move, it got tapped or bashed depending on what mood I was in, the dog was forever keeping out of the way. We did have a pet tortoise that wasn't so lucky though.

By now it was pretty common knowledge with family and friends that I was obsessed with drumming, even though I still didn't have a real drum to wallop. A friend of dad's in the club had heard that the North Ormesby Brass Band were looking for a big bass drum player. My dad said, "Well he's not that big really, but I'm sure he'll be able to hit a bass drum. Might stop him knocking fuck out of everything else in the house."

I went to see them and they let me have a go and

took me on. I loved it, but the highlight had to be the day we performed at Ayresome Park in front of a full house when Middlesbrough played against Birmingham City. We marched up and down the pitch and, at one point, as we approached the end of the pitch, some of the band peeled off to the left and some of the band peeled off to the right. Not me though, I was right in the middle of the back line and could see fuck all over the top of my bass drum, so I carried on straight a few steps more and walked right into one of the fucking goalposts. You'd think the teams had just come out by the way the crowd roared with fucking laughter, made the local newspaper anyway. I heard some clever twat shout out, "He's hit the post… sign him on!"

After that, I was hooked. Got myself a set of drums and was lucky enough to get a job playing in the Station Hotel at Redcar. The Ritz, it wasn't, but hey I was suddenly in show business, backing the resident pianist, Nancy Pinkley. She wasn't in the first throws of spring but when it came to playing the piano she was a true professional. That was at the beginning of the evening, by the end of the night she was playing the piano like Houdini, as though she was in a straightjacket with handcuffs on. You see, she liked a good drink. Guinness was her tipple and she'd sink around eight pints a night, then fart so fucking loud that the lads in the bar thought I'd put in an extra loud drum roll. We played there every Saturday night. It was the roughest place in town, but it didn't bother Nancy, she was always too pissed to notice. There were times when I had to tell her that the lid was still down on her piano, even though we were halfway through a number. The crowd never noticed, they were always looking around deciding who was next to get filled in. My drum kit regularly got used as a weapon.

One thing led to another, and my two cousins, Dec and Lee, both Vaseys, had formed a group called Pipeline and they thought it would be a good idea if I joined them. By this time I'd been playing drums around a few pub venues in the area and had got cocky enough to stand up and tell a few jokes. I still wasn't sure if anyone was supposed to laugh back, but I didn't give a fuck anyway, so I still made them listen to me. I'd go and watch other comedians. My favourite, at the time, was Johnny Hammond who had a big following in the local clubs. I loved his cheeky grin and warm approach, and wished I could be just like him, never thinking that, one day, we'd become the best of friends. Johnny inspired me to work more on my comedy side whilst still playing the drums. One of my earliest efforts was: a traffic warden said, "You can't park there, fatty." I said, "I'm looking for a shithouse." He said, "You've found one."

It wasn't long before Pipeline became Dec Vasey's Four Man Band, and the whole of our first spot each night was a mixture of comedy and music. I think we were probably one of the first comedy show-groups working the North East club circuit. Fuck me, once you've worked in those clubs you could go anywhere. Some get etched onto your brain forever like Redhouse Social and Hylton Castle, both in Sunderland, The Bloodtub in Stockton and too many more to name. Getting paid-off because we were trying to do something a bit different to the norm was becoming a fucking habit, but we were all having a great time, so we just thought fuck 'em. Yes, you had to be either thick skinned or just plain thick to want to make a living entertaining in those clubs.

Gradually the stand-up comedy part of the act became more prominent when we formed the comedy show, Allcock and Brown. We performed up and down the country, still getting paid off occasionally. We weren't everyone's cup of tea. When Allcock and Brown disbanded it was the birth of Roy Chubby Brown. It was true to say that the majority of workingmen's clubs and nightclubs weren't quite ready for the style of Chubby's fucking and blinding quite yet. Undeterred, I still wasn't in the mood to be told what I could say and what I couldn't say. Mind you, expressing my delight at the size of the Mayor's wife's tits at a local gig might not have been one of my best career decisions, paid off and barred from appearing in the club again was the result of that indiscretion.

Eventually the act progressed to concert halls where

the audiences who came were fully aware of the type of comedy they were going to witness and I could fuck, cunt, twat, bastard and shite to my heart's content. Well, not shite, but you know what I mean. They loved it and came back for more, for which I'm eternally grateful, and I'm indebted to my loyal fans that have supported me throughout the years.

So, in a nutshell, that's how the big bass drummer in the Boy's Brigade, who walked into the goalpost at Ayresome Park those many years ago, grew up to become Roy Chubby Brown. In fact you could do the same if you gave it a try, just get yourself a fucking big drum and give it an enormous twat with a stick… you can't beat it!

'Not such a little drummer boy, after all.'

THERE'S NO BUSINESS LIKE IT (SHOWBIZ, THAT IS)

When Posh Spice dies, how will they know?
Miserable cunt.

Piers Morgan is so unpopular the phone wouldn't even ring to stop him enjoying a bath.

Jordan's been ill… don't worry, she'll be back on her knees in no time.

Jordan says stuff on the internet is fake news… they must be talking about her tits.

Been talent spotted this morning…
by Embarrassing Bodies.
They told me I could have my own show…
cheeky bastards.

A ventriloquist was talking to his agent about there not being much work coming in and his agent said, "Well, old time ventriloquists are becoming a thing of the past, you should think about trying to do something else."

The ventriloquist said, "Like what?"

The agent said, "What about becoming a medium? You know like contacting the dead for people. Doris Stokes used to do it but she's not around anymore. Train up on it, must be worth giving it a try."

"Okay," said the ventriloquist, "I've got nothing to lose."

So the ventriloquist went away and learned everything he needed to know about becoming a medium. Three weeks later he'd got his own office and was welcoming his first customer… a little old lady.

The little old lady said to the ventriloquist, "I've never been to see a medium before, what do I get for my money?"

The ventriloquist said, "Well I've got three different priced sittings. Firstly for ten pounds, I can arrange for you to speak to your loved one that's gone before. Secondly for twenty pounds, I can arrange for you to speak to your loved one that's gone before and for them to speak back to you. Finally, not only can I arrange for you to speak to your loved one that's gone before and for them to speak back to you, but at the same time I'll drink a glass of water."

When I first bought a Yamaha piano and I sat down to play it, I was that shit the company sent two great big Japanese blokes around to rub the name off it, and then they beat me up.

This song is a folk song… when I sing it people say, "Oh folk!"

The dressing room was so small
I saw a Daddy Short Legs.

I used to be in variety, but I don't make a song and dance about it.

"Excuse me, how do you get to The Albert Hall?"

"With lots of practice, mate."

The male stripper was so good that one of the women had a stroke.

THINGS I CAN'T STAND

When the salt pot top comes off
and drowns your chips.

Women who fart and don't say, "I'm sorry."

When you ask someone the time
and they just shrug their shoulders.

When you see your ex-wife in a new car.

Fanny fucking farrrrts!!! You're not listening are you?

DOCTOR I'M IN TROUBLE

He might not be a brain surgeon,
but you should see him operate.

For what good these suppositories are,
I might just as well shove them up my arse.

Doctor said, "You need to cut down on your smoking, Chubby. Try just having one after each meal."

After a week I was down to twenty meals a day.

The doctor rang this morning and told me that he thought the wife wasn't too clever, which is a slight improvement really because I always thought she was as thick as fuck.

I could have been a doctor
but I didn't have the patience.

Went to the medical centre and the doctor said to the wife, "You look terrible."

I turned to her and said, "I told you so."

Exercise kills germs... didn't know germs could exercise.

There's a new patch out to stop you eating too much... fits over your mouth.

My willy feels a bit stiff... think it needs a massage.

Doctor said, "Haven't seen you for ages, Mr. Brown."

I said, "I know, Doctor, I've been ill."

Going to the doctor's these days is a bit like going to a brothel... you tend to wait around much longer than you're in there. Er... so they say.

HOME SWEET HOME

There are that many break-ins where we live that if you close a window you're likely to trap someone's fingers in it.

😀

This time every year my next-door neighbour asks me to trim her bush. Can be quite thorny, especially if she doesn't get her bush trimmed.

😂

My cousin has just got a job as a leaf blower for the council, but my old nan keeps telling everybody he's got a blowjob.

😆

We were so poor that the Red Cross used to send us parcels.

😜

The police handcuffed the wife. I said to the copper the last time we did that she charged me a £100 for sex.

My mam used to send us out to
sell pegs to the gypsies.

"Landlord, our living room's very draughty."

"Well it is built out of breezeblock."

"Mam, do you want me to go out to play again
while you pay the milkman?"

"Grandad, you're sleeping with a
seventeen year old girl, it could be fatal."

"Well, if she dies, she fucking dies, Chubbs."

Our mam said our dad was the nicest
bloke she'd ever met, and that she would
like to meet him again some time.

Grandad said, "Couldn't sleep last night. There was this light that kept going on and off and on and off."

I turned to the wife and said, "At last, we've found out who keeps pissing in the fridge."

My kids were that horrible
Santa Claus refused to see them.

My sixteen year old daughter said, "I'm pregnant, dad, but I'll get compensation."

I said, "You won't get compensation for being pregnant."

She said, "I will, it was an accident and it happened at work."

THINGS I CAN'T STAND

When they name a disease after you.

When the doctor tells you to kiss it better
and you know it's piles.

Trying to masturbate and hold a mucky picture
at the same time.

Getting a standing ovation at a dwarves only concert.

When the machine that's keeping
your wife alive is the fridge.

Fucking, bastard, twatting fanny farrrrts!
I've told you three times already!

LITTLE OLD ME

I was dead unlucky with girls at school.
The only time I got a girl to meet me behind
the bike sheds, she told me she was on her
cycle. I said, "Well just park it with the others
and get yer knickers off."

I'm about as unlucky as
Pinocchio looking for no strings sex.

I built my own house…
it wasn't till I was told the attic was flooded
that I realised I'd had the plans upside down.

First thing I say to a girl in bed is,
"Am I squashing you, pet?"

Went to give blood and the nurse said, Just a small prick, Mr. Brown."

I said, "Has my wife been in here?"

The wife wrote a book 'How to look thin… stand next to my husband.'

I know I'm big but I think it's a bit much when I walked into the restaurant and the waiter shouted through to the kitchen, "We'll have to kill another cow!"

I always back scuttle the wife… I don't want her getting in my view of the telly.

I went to a concert at the weekend… it was a bit strange. The guitarist kept turning round and fiddling with his amplifier, turning it up one minute then down the next. The lead singer kept moving his microphone stand backwards and forwards until he got it in the right position. I tell you, it's the last fucking time I go to see OCDC.

With a face like mine you don't need a vasectomy.

Was I an ugly baby? The woman next door
had to breastfeed me.

I wish I'd been the Pope at the airport,
bet they didn't look up his fucking arse.

I've fucked Siamese twins. While one was
giving me a blowjob, my balls were dangling
in the other one's eyes.

Never felt wanted as a child…
my parents used to take me
to play in the quicksand.

I was filling in a form yesterday… where it said
male or female, I put 'don't know', because
I stand up for a slash but still get called a cunt.

Got chased by an elephant the other week…
my own fault for looking like a fucking iced bun.

I'm so unlucky that if I killed myself,
God would send me a bill.

I was at a funeral this morning. A friend of mine's
wife had died. He made a very moving speech…
spent twenty minutes complaining about her driving.

When I've been on a diet,
I'm sure even my ears can smell food.

I've been asked to appear in a new musical film about
crossdressers in prison… it's called 'Jailhouse Frock'.

At school I was always late. I must have been
the only one in our class who brought a note
when I turned up on time.

Many thanks for taking the time to finger through a load of old cracks. As my Great Grandad used to always tell me, when he was a resident at The Seaview Nursing Home, he got a great deal of pleasure from fingering old cracks.